MINI MAKES

Handmade Home

MORE THAN 25 GORGEOUS
IDEAS FOR THE HOME

 | Penguin Random House

Project Editor Elizabeth Yeates
Designer Alison Gardner
Senior Jacket Creative Mark Penfound
Pre-Production Producer Andy Hilliard
Producer Konrad Kirkham
Special Sales Creative Project Manager
Alison Donovan

First published in Great Britain in 2015 by
Dorling Kindersley Limited,
80 Strand, London WC2R 0RL

Material previously published in
Handmade Gifts (2013)

Copyright © 2013, 2015 Dorling Kindersley Limited
A Penguin Random House Company
001 – 284144 – Mar/15

A CIP catalogue record for this book
is available from the British Library.
ISBN 978-0-2412-0093-3

Printed in China

All images © Dorling Kindersley Limited
For further information see: **www.dkimages.com**

A WORLD OF IDEAS:
SEE ALL THERE IS TO KNOW

Contents

Introduction

Sometimes a box of chocolates or another pair
of socks simply won't do. For a truly thoughtful
present, making your own gifts is the way forward:
you can create something beautiful, unique, and
affordable, regardless of whether you have an hour
or two to spend or an afternoon.

Every idea in *Handmade Home* is explained in step-by-step
photographs so you can be sure that your gift will have a
professional finish, and will be well worth the time you invest.
If the project needs a template, we include one so you know it
will work. There are lots of ideas for how you can add your own
twist, so you can make the gift that is exactly right for the
person you have in mind.

We have included a range of gift ideas, each requiring
different levels of skill and time. We hope you have a
wonderful time making your gifts... and that you find
time to make something for yourself!

For the home

Customized cushion

Customize a plain cushion cover with appliqué fabric shapes, buttons, and decorative stitches to make a stylish or funky cushion at a low cost – a perfect gift for a new home or for a child's bedroom.

....

To make a blossom cushion you will need

Tools: washable ink pen • tracing paper • steam iron • dressmaker's scissors • sewing pins • sewing machine • sewing needle • cotton sewing threads

Materials: iron-on interfacing • brown cotton fabric • white cotton fabric • pink floral cotton fabric • green felt • cushion cover • 8 small white buttons and 4 large white buttons

1

Enlarge the blossom cushion templates on p.114 to fit your cushion. Trace all the shapes apart from the leaves onto iron-on interfacing.

2

Cut out the interfacing and iron each piece onto the chosen fabric for each: brown cotton for the bird and branch, white cotton for 12 petals, and pink floral cotton for 12 centres.

 3

Carefully cut out all
the interfaced shapes.

 4

Trace the leaf template onto paper and cut it out.
Use the template to trace and cut out six leaves
from the felt. There is no need to iron these onto
interfacing as felt will not fray.

 6

Machine sew the branch and bird onto
the cushion using a contrasting colour
cotton thread, carefully sewing about
3–5mm (¹/₈–¼in) from the edges.

 7

Match the large, white flowers with the large,
pink centres and the small, white flowers with
the small, pink centres. Place the flowers and
leaves onto the cushion and pin in position.

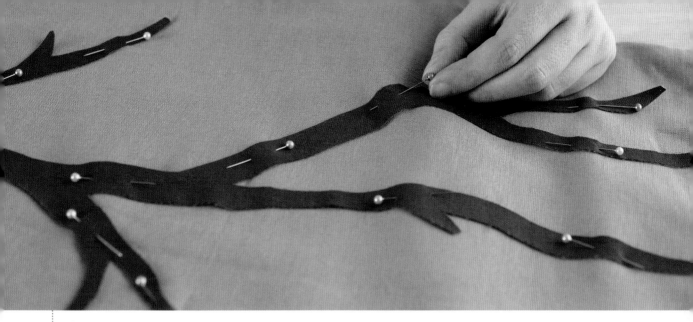

 5

Place the cushion cover on a flat surface and place the branch and bird in position. Pin or use tacking stitches to secure.

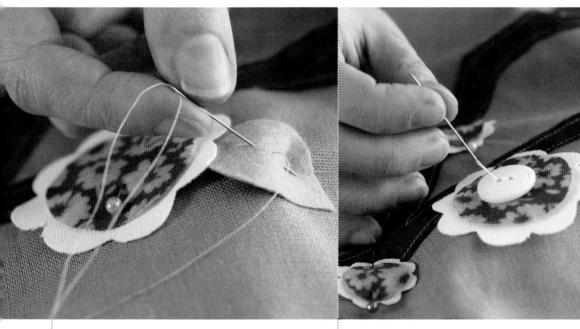

 8

Tuck some of the leaves behind the flowers to create a natural effect. Hand sew the leaves on in a matching cotton down the centres, using four or five backstitches to secure.

 9

Sew large and small buttons into the centres of the flowers, sewing through the cushion cover to secure the flowers to the cover.

Castle cushion

Be as creative as you like with this castle. Start with the template on p.116 to create the basic shape. Use leather-effect fabric for the drawbridge and windows, and a favourite colour for the flag. The prince and princess are made from felt offcuts and are attached to the cushion by thin cord so they cannot be lost! You can make your own, or add ready-made fabric dolls. Remember to make a few pockets in the design for them to go into.

Tip: Use the templates on p.117 to make the dolls. Add yarn for hair and sew or draw the faces.

Skull and crossbones cushion

A fun skull motif will appeal to children of all ages, particularly those with a love of pirates! Find the template for this project on p.115. Cut out the skull and crossbone shapes from black felt and tack into position on the cushion cover Machine sew around the edge of the black shapes using white cotton. Cut out eyes and teeth from white felt and sew them by hand into position, onto the skull.

Guitar cushion

This is the perfect cushion for a teenager's room. Using the template on p.115, cut out the shapes for the guitar from black and white felt or suede-effect fabric. Tack and stitch the guitar body into place first, using contrast thread. Add the white board section, sewing it on with white thread. Add the black details, again using contrast thread. Use white ribbon for the strings, and stitch into position. A drum or a section of piano keys would also look effective.

Dot-decorated
ceramics

Painting ceramics by hand can seem a bit daunting, but this dot-decorating method is virtually foolproof. Almost any line-drawing can be turned into a dot painting, so once you have mastered the technique try out your own designs.

To make a dot-decorated vase you will need

Tools: scissors • ballpoint pen

Materials: ceramic vase • baby wipes or damp cloth • red transfer paper
• masking tape • black, food-safe ceramic pen or paint in a dispenser

1

Clean the vase to remove any loose dust or grease from the surface. Photocopy the vase template (see p.118) and reduce or enlarge it to fit.

2

Place a sheet of transfer paper behind the template and cut out the main dandelion motif. Then cut out the individual seeds.

3

Tape the dandelion template to the front of your vase, with the transfer paper underneath. Position the seeds around the template and on one adjoining side.

4

Using a ballpoint pen, firmly trace the design onto the vase. Use solid lines across the dots as these show up best.

7

Using the template as a guide, complete the design with dots. Keep the spacing of the dots even and work quickly to avoid the paint pooling. Paint short, solid lines at the ends of the seeds and then fill in the dots.

5

Remove the template and check that the lines are visible. If not, wipe away the trace lines and repeat the process, pressing down more firmly.

6

Use a ceramic paint pen or paint in a dispenser to draw the stem of the dandelion in one continuous line.

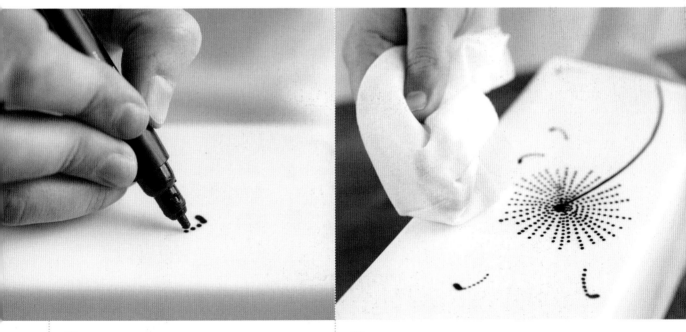

8

Repeat Steps 4–7 to decorate the second side of the vase. Let the paint dry before repeating the whole process for the remaining two sides.

9

When the paint is completely dry, use a baby wipe or damp cloth to wipe off the trace lines. Follow the paint manufacturer's instructions to set the paint.

Mug and coaster set

Create this delicately patterned mug and coaster
set in exactly the same way as the vase (see
pp.14–17) using the mug and coaster template
(see p.119). When painting the dots, remember
to work from left to right (right to left if you're
left-handed) across the pattern to avoid
smudging the dots you have already made.

} *Tip: Create a set of mugs
using the same design in
different colours — one for
each family member.*

Celebration bunting plate

As a rule, it is not safe to eat food from hand-painted ceramics (but do check the label on your paints). The dot-decorating method can be used to create stunning display plates though, and this bunting plate is the perfect gift to mark a celebration. Use the template (see p.119) to transfer the pattern to the plate. Draw the black lines, let them dry, then work across the pattern filling in the flags with coloured dots.

}*Tip: Add a celebratory message or the recipients name to the plate by painting a letter in each flag.*

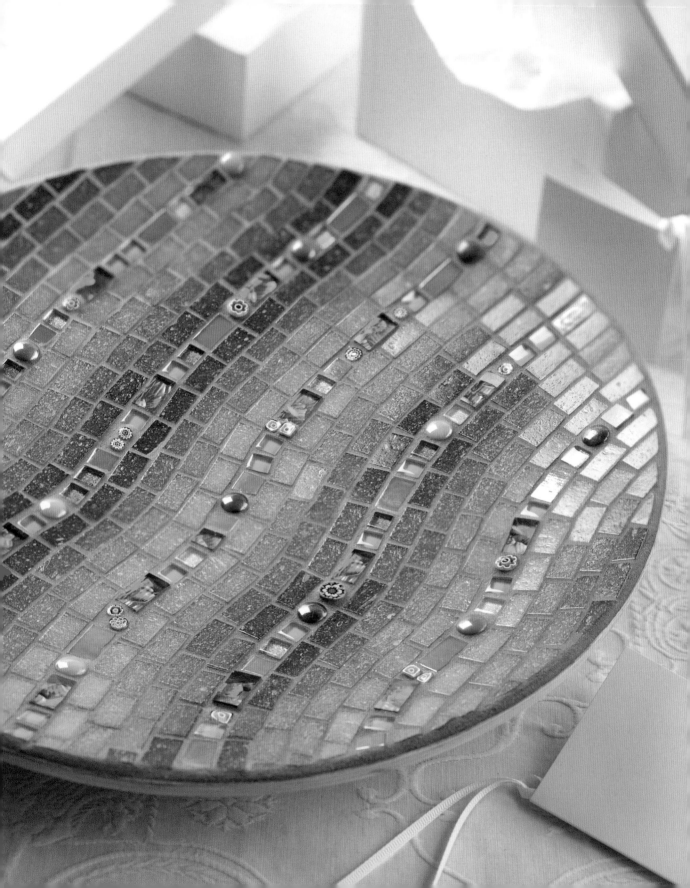

Mosaic bowl

This calming, woodland-inspired mosaic bowl is created using the direct method, meaning that tiles are glued straight onto the object and then grouted. This will not produce a completely level surface, resulting in a tactile bowl.

To make a mosaic bowl you will need

Tools: tile nippers • rubber gloves • protective mask & goggles • grout spreader • sponge • lint-free cloth

Materials: wooden bowl • tesserae in different shades of green • flat-backed beads and 5mm millefiori • PVA glue • mosaic grout (either pre-mixed or made up following the manufacturer's instructions)

1

Draw a wavy line onto your bowl, about 4.5cm (1¾in) from the rim. Draw a second line roughly 1.5cm (⅝in) below this one. This will be the first accent line on your bowl.

2

Prepare your tiles by soaking or peeling off any backing sheets. Select the plain tiles and those for the accent lines, and place them in groups of the same colour and type.

 3

Cut tiles for the accent lines. Wearing goggles, hold the tile between thumb and forefinger and, positioning nippers at the edge, gently squeeze. Repeat to cut into quarters.

 4

Arrange the tiles and embellishments between your wavy lines. Vary iridescent and matt tiles, as well as round and rectangular ones to create a pattern.

 7

Complete one line at a time, increasing or decreasing the shade and adding accent lines at regular intervals. When complete, leave to dry overnight.

 8

Wearing rubber gloves and a mask, apply the grout generously to the mosaic, working in different directions. Make sure to also grout around the outer edge of the bowl.

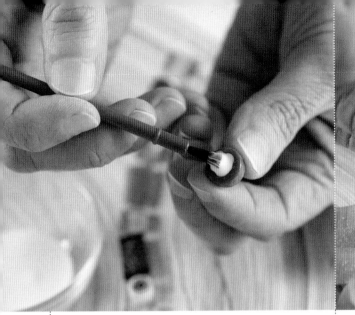

5

Move the pieces off the line, keeping their order. Add a dab of glue to the back of each piece and stick them to your bowl leaving even gaps between them.

6

For the lines of plain tiles, start with the lightest green tiles, and cut them in half (see Step 3). Glue them either side of the accent line, trimming them if necessary.

9

Use a damp sponge to carefully wipe away the excess grout. Leave for 20 minutes, then, before the grout is hard, wipe gently again.

10

When the grout is completely dry, use a lint-free dry cloth to wipe away any residue and polish the tiles to a shine.

Owl jewellery box

You will need
Wooden box
Glazed and unglazed ceramic tiles
Glass nuggets and beads
White grout
Felt for base

This pretty jewellery box is made using the same technique as the mosaic bowl on pp.20–23. Start by drawing an owl template design on the box and then seal the box with watered-down PVA glue. Start filling in the design, attaching the nuggets and whole tiles first. Cut the remaining tiles to size to complete the design. Finally, fill in the area around the design with randomly cut tiles – a technique known as crazy paving. Allow to dry and then grout the lid. Grout the box one side at a time, waiting for each side to dry before starting the next. Glue felt to the base to finish the box.

Flower garland mirror

You will need
Mirror with wide, flat, wooden frame
A selection of tiles and glass nuggets
White grout

Make this mirror in the same way as the mosaic bowl on pp.20–23. Draw on the a flower design and seal the wooden frame with watered-down PVA glue if necessary. Create the flowers first, starting with a nugget and using tile nippers to shape the petals. Next, make the leaf garlands. Fill in the gaps with crazy paving (see above), and use tile halves to fill in the outer edge of the border. Cover the mirror with masking tape to protect it when grouting. Grout the frame, ensuring you create a straight edge around the mirror.

Round tea light holder

You will need
Ball-shaped, wooden tea light holder
Old crockery, broken into small pieces
Tiles and glass nuggets
White grout
Felt for the base

This tea light holder is made in the same way as the mosaic bowl (see pp.20–23), but using fragments of broken crockery. First, draw your design on the tea light holder and then seal it with watered-down PVA glue. Glue down the nuggets first, and then use tile nippers to shape the crockery pieces into petals. Next, add any whole tiles. Finally, fill in the area around the design with more crockery pieces. Work a small area at a time. Some tiles may have to be held in place using tape until they dry. Grout, allow to dry, and attach felt to the base to finish.

Seaside coasters

You will need
MDF squares
Tiles in a variety of colours
Grey grout

These seaside-inspired coasters have been made out of squares of MDF, using the technique described for the mosaic bowl on pp.20–23. Draw your own design, first draw guidelines onto the coaster in pencil. Fill in the design first, shaping the tiles to fit. Try to keep the tiles fairly flat, as you will need to be able to rest a glass or mug on the coaster when finished. Next, fill in the background using square tiles, shaping them to fit as necessary. Again, try to keep the tiles as flat as possible. Grout the coasters, not forgetting the edges, to finish.

Rollaway gameboard

This draughts board has an integrated pocket for game pieces and it rolls up neatly, making it easy to store and ideal for travel. The patchwork top is cleverly made from fabric strips, saving you having to piece each square separately.

To make a rollaway gameboard you will need

Tools: dressmaker's scissors • sewing machine • sewing pins • iron

Materials: plain fabric in brown and cream • decorative fabric in two different designs • cotton sewing thread • interfacing • 3cm (1¼in) button • thin ribbon • buttons in 2 colours to use as draught pieces

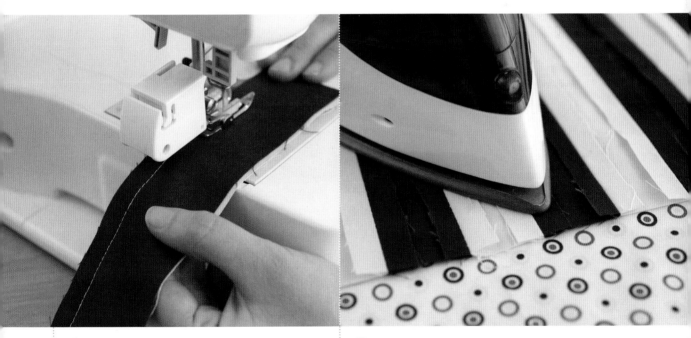

1
Use the chart in the Templates section (p.117) to measure and cut out the fabric pieces. Sew together one light and one dark strip with a 1cm (⅜in) seam allowance.

2
Sew a light strip to the other edge of the first dark strip. Add the remaining strips one at a time, alternating colours. Press all the seams open, forming a 29cm (12in) wide piece.

3

Mark lines across the strips every 5cm (2in). Cut along the lines to make eight bands. Pin the bands together, offsetting every other row by one square to make a chequerboard.

4

Sew the strips together with a 1cm (⅜in) seam allowance. Press open the seams. Trim off the extra squares on either side to create an 8 x 8 board, leaving the seam allowance.

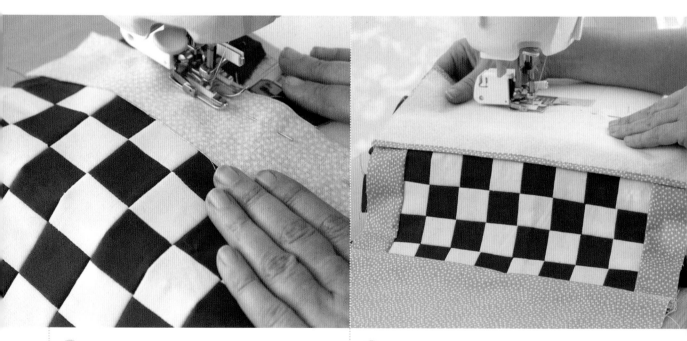

7

Place the two narrow strips of inner fabric at two opposite sides of the board, right side to right side. Pin, then sew with a 1cm (⅜in) seam allowance. Press the seams open.

8

Sew the two remaining inner fabric panels to the two remaining edges of the board with a 1cm (⅜in) seam allowance. Press the seams away from the board.

5

Apply interfacing to the wrong side of the 30 x 50cm (12 x 20in) piece of outer fabric and one of the 30 x 14cm (12 x 5¾in) pieces of inner fabric.

6

Fold over a 5mm (¼in) double hem at one end of the interfaced outer fabric and stitch. Do the same along one long edge of the interfaced inner fabric. These will form the pocket edges.

9

Place the right side of the outer fabric and the right side of the inner fabric together, making sure the pocket hems (see step 6) line up. Pin, then sew with 1cm (⅜in) seam allowance along three sides, leaving the pocket edges open.

10

Overstitch along the edge of the chequerboard closest to the pocket edges to form an interlined pocket. You can use the pocket to store the game pieces.

11

Sew a 3cm (1¼in) button in the middle of the outside of the non-pocket end, approximately 1.5cm (⅝in) from the edge. Thread a thin ribbon through the buttonhole.

12

Tie a knot in the ribbon behind the button. Wrap the ribbon around the rolled-up game, securing the counters inside. Secure the roll by winding the ribbon around the button.

All of these bags are made in the same way as the wave-patterned bag on pp.33–35. Turn to pp.36–37 for further instructions, ideas, and inspiration.

Stencilled bags

Turn plain canvas bags into unique and personal fashion statements with the use of paper stencils and fabric paint. Once you can stencil with confidence, why not try decorating a T-shirt or cushion cover?

To make the wave-patterned bag you will need

Tools: pencil • scalpel • cutting mat • iron • masking tape • plate or palette • sponge • hairdryer • kitchen towel

Materials: tracing paper • stencil paper or card • fabric bag • scrap paper or newspaper • fabric paint in two colours

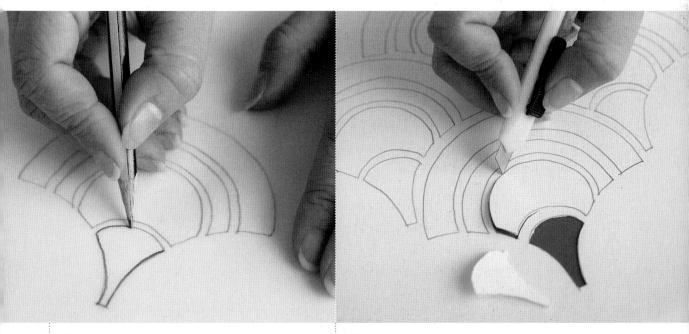

1

Trace the stencil template from p.121 on to tracing paper. Transfer it onto card by flipping the tracing paper over and drawing over the lines while pressing down firmly.

2

Use a scalpel to carefully cut the stencil shape out. If making a repeat pattern, you can cut out the stencil shape a number of times on one sheet, making sure to leave a border of paper.

 33

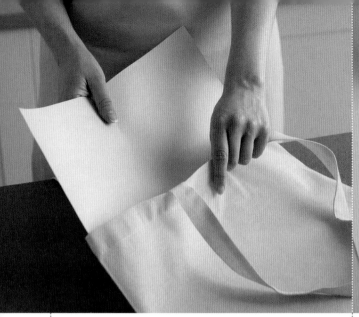

3

Prepare your fabric bag by ironing it, and line the inside with scrap paper or newspaper to stop any excess ink that may soak through the fabric from running through to the back of the bag.

4

Tape down the stencil. Pour some paint on a plate or palette. Dip a clean, dry sponge in the paint, dabbing off any excess. Then apply the paint with the sponge, starting from the centre and working out.

6

Use kitchen towel to blot your stencil and let it dry. You can also prepare more stencils, allowing you to move on with the design while you wait for the first stencil to dry.

7

Once your stencil and fabric paint are dry, reposition your stencil on the bag. Repeat the application process as many times as desired, leaving a few gaps for the second colour.

5

Remove your stencil and put it to one side to dry. Use a hairdryer to dry the paint onto the fabric, ensuring you blow dry the inside of your fabric bag as well as the front so the paint doesn't dry to the lining paper.

8

Once you've stencilled all of the design in one colour and it has dried, apply the second colour in the same way as the first, using a new stencil. Leave to dry overnight.

9

When the fabric paint has fully dried, iron the fabric for a minute or two to fix the paint to the material. You may wish to use a cloth to protect your iron.

 35

Fluttering butterflies

This bag has been stencilled in the same way as the wave-patterned bag on pp.33–35, using the templates on p.121. Butterflies of different shapes and sizes are positioned at slight angles on the same diagonal line, making it look like they are all fluttering in the same direction. Creating the same stencil in different sizes, and overlapping some of the images, also adds a sense of depth to the scene.

The same colour paint has been used to create these butterflies, but you could try stencilling them in a variety of colours for a different look. Alternatively, wait for the design to dry and paint or stencil different coloured markings on the butterflies.

Stitched bag

This large-scale design looks like thread that has been stitched onto the bag, attached to a needle that has also been pushed through the fabric. The look is achieved by creating gaps in the stencil design where the item or object would be obscured by the fabric. Follow the instructions on pp.33–35 to create this look, using the stencils on p.120. Remember to cut separate stencils for different-coloured elements.

Have fun playing with the blank canvas provided by the bag by thinking of other designs that could be interacting with it in some way. For example, you could stencil on a belt going through belt loops, or a ribbon "threaded" through the bag.

Repeated chevrons

This deceptively simple idea results in a striking design with an element of optical illusion. Using the template on p.120, create a stencil, cutting several chevron shapes at equal distances to each other. Following the instructions for the wave-patterned bag on pp.33–35 and starting in the centre of your bag, stencil the pattern onto the bag and dry it. Reposition the stencil so that it continues the chevron pattern as shown, pointing the chevrons the opposite way for every other column, and taking care to keep all the stencilled figures evenly spaced.

Any evenly spaced, repeated pattern makes a striking design, so try this with circles or triangles for a different look. You could also try varying the colours, either according to a pattern or randomly.

Pencil illusion

At first glance it looks like these pencils are complete, but on closer inspection, you can see that only the tip and shaft of the pencil have been stencilled onto the bag. Your eye fills in the rest, completing the image with the background colour. This is a great technique to use for stencilled designs as it can be difficult to stencil very narrow lines or other details needed to complete an image. To make these pencils, use the stencil template on p.120 and follow the instructions for the wave-patterned bag on pp.33–35.

Make a sleeve for a device of any size by following the instructions for the tablet protector on pp.39–41. Choose the correct-size button to finish it off.

Phone and tablet
protectors

Make a stylish and individual slipcase for a gadget-lover's phone, tablet, or laptop. These instructions are based on the individual device's measurements, and so can be used to make a cover for any make or model.

To make a tablet protector you will need

Tools: tape measure • dressmaker's scissors • iron • ruler • fabric marker • sewing pins • sewing machine or needle
Materials: cotton fabric for the shell • lining fabric • fleece fabric • medium-weight, fusible, woven interfacing
• 15cm (5⅞in) round elastic • button • cotton sewing thread

1
Use a tape measure to measure around the length of the device. Divide this number by two, and then add 4.5cm (1¾in). Do the same for the width of the device.

2
Using the measurements from Step 1, draw and cut two rectangles from your chosen shell fabric. Then do the same for the lining fabric, fleece fabric, and fusible woven interfacing.

3

Iron one piece of fusible interfacing to the wrong side of each piece of shell fabric. With the wrong sides facing, lightly iron the lining fabric to the fleece fabric from the side of the lining.

4

Mark a sewing line 1cm (⅜in) from the edge along all four edges of one of the interfaced pieces, on the side of the interfacing. Do the same for one of the fleece and lining pieces, on the fleece side.

7

Pin the two padded lining pieces together, lining sides facing, marking a 12cm (4¾in) gap along the bottom edge. Sew as in Step 6, leaving a gap. Trim the seams and overstitch the edges.

8

Turn the shell right side out and press. Mark the centre of the top sewing line, mark down 5cm (2in), and sew on the button. Turn wrong side out, add a sewing line to the other side, and mark its centre for the elastic.

5

Round out the bottom corners of each of the pieces that you have drawn sewing lines on, using a button as a template, and drawing around the button.

6

Pin the two interfaced pieces together, right sides facing and top edges matching. Sew down one side, across the bottom, and up the other side, along the line. Trim the seams and overstitch the edges.

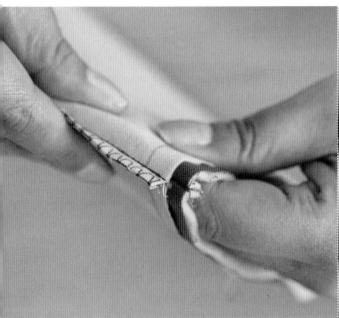

9

Turn the lining right side out. Slide it inside the outer piece. Insert the elastic loop between the two pieces as marked. Pin and sew around the sewing line, double-stitching over the elastic.

10

Trim the seam and overstitch the edges. Reach through the opening in the bottom lining to turn the cover right side out. Stitch closed the gap in the lining by hand. Press the cover.

Personalized journal

For the home

What better place to store notes and thoughts than in a handmade journal with a personalized cover? This technique demands precision – each stage leads on to the next, so if you're slightly "out", the journal may look misshapen.

To make a journal you will need

Tools: bone folder • craft knife • pencil • metal ruler • self-healing cutting mat • sewing needle
Materials: 6 sheets of heavy A3 white or cream paper • 1 sheet of A3 decorative paper • white thread

1
Making sure that the grain is running vertically, fold each piece of white or cream A3 paper in half so that the short edges meet. Smooth the crease with the bone folder.

2
Starting from the inside of the folded sheet, cut along the fold with the knife, stopping at a point just over halfway along the fold.

3

Fold each sheet of paper in half again, short edge to short edge. Crease then cut along the fold, stopping just after halfway. Fold the paper in half again, short edge to short edge, and crease.

4

Assemble the folded sheets in a pile of "stacks". To make the cover, first fold the decorative paper in half so that the long edges meet and press the crease down with the bone folder.

7

Use the ruler and the bone folder to crease the cover along the second pencil line you have just drawn. The area between the two creases will be the spine of your journal.

8

Measure the height of the cover, and divide this distance into five equal sections. Mark each section on the spine, and then use a craft knife to cut a slit through each line.

 5

Fold the paper in half again, this time so that the short edges meet. Smooth down the crease with the bone folder.

 6

Open the cover and draw a line down the crease. Press down gently on the pile of stacks and measure the height of the pile. Then measure the same distance to one side of the crease. Draw a line.

9

Use the ruler to draw lines on the pile of paper stacks to correspond with the slits in the cover.

 10

Open up each paper segment and prick the needle through each mark. There should now be four evenly spaced holes in each paper segment. Thread the needle.

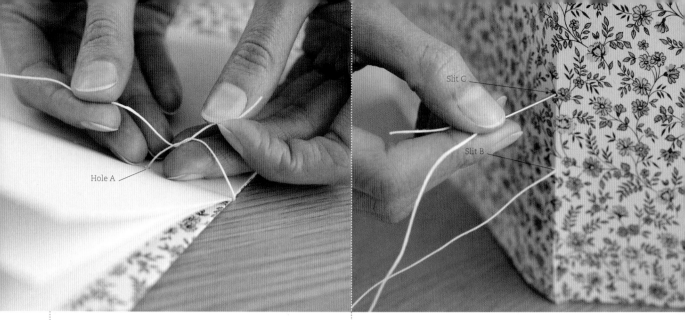

 11

With one stack on top of the cover, push the needle through the first hole (hole A) and first slit (slit A) from the inside. Pass the thread around the top of the spine and tie a knot.

12

Pass the needle through the hole B from the inside and out through slit B. Run the thread along the spine and push the needle in through slit C and hole C to the inside.

 15

Add a new stack and continue, securing and adding stacks. After the last stack, pass the needle around the top of the journal, and below one of the stitches. Knot on the inside.

16

Fold the decorative paper back over the stack and smooth it down, creasing the fold with your finger.

Hole D

Slit D

Hole 2D

Slit D

Hole D

13

Push the needle out through hole D and slit D. Looping the thread around the bottom of the spine, push the needle through just hole D again. Tighten the thread.

14

Add the next stack. Go through the first hole of the new stack (hole 2D) to the inside, then around the bottom of the spine and back through slit D and hole 2D. Continue, securing the second stack like the first.

17

Now fold the paper under again to form the jacket. Repeat for the other side.

18

Cut through the edges of the pages of the first stack. Repeat for all the other stacks.

Ribbon-bound
photo album

This wonderful album is bound to become a family treasure. Use thick, acid-free card for the pages to protect your photographs and thick, good-quality ribbon to ensure that the binding holds for years to come.

To make a ribbon-bound photo album you will need

Tools: craft knife • metal ruler • self-healing cutting mat • bookbinding needle

Materials: sheets of heavy white or cream paper • 3 x 15cm (5⅞in) lengths of ribbon • masking tape • 3 x 1m (40in) linen bookbinding thread • 2 sheets 2–3mm (¹⁄₁₆–⅛in) cardboard • 2 sheets decorative paper • glue • greaseproof paper

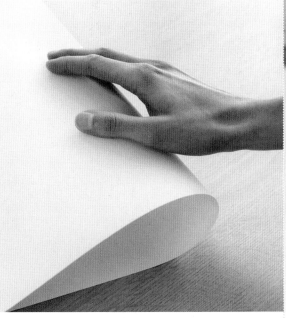

1

Find the grain of the paper by folding it over lengthways and widthways. The fold with least resistance tells you that the grain runs up and down.

2

With the grain running vertically, use the template (see p.122) to cut 18 rectangles to make 15 pages, two end papers, and one sewing template.

3

Transfer the hole markings to one sheet to use as your sewing template. One at a time, line up each of the 15 pages with the sewing template and pierce the needle through each mark.

4

Place one page at the edge of a table, the pierced side lined up with the table edge. Position the three lengths of ribbon between each set of holes, and tape them to the edge of the table.

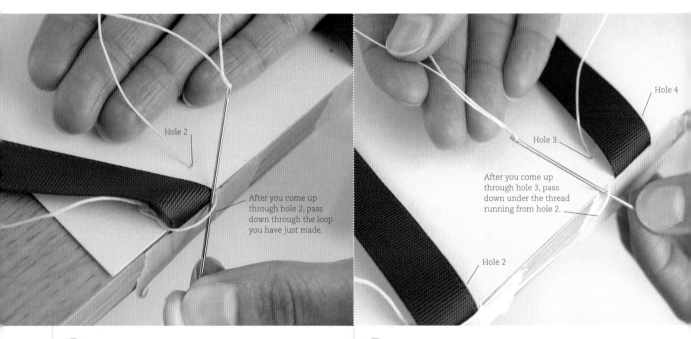

Hole 2

After you come up through hole 2, pass down through the loop you have just made.

Hole 4

Hole 3

After you come up through hole 3, pass down under the thread running from hole 2.

Hole 2

7

After you come up through the second hole, flip the ribbons over the paper. Pass down through the loop you have just made. Take care not to pull too tight, keeping all the loops slightly loose.

8

Next pass through hole 3, bottom to top, then under the thread running from hole 2. Pass through hole 4, bottom to top, and through the loop you have just made (see Step 7).

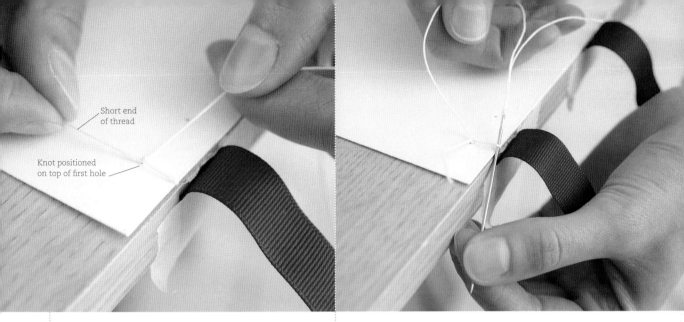

Short end
of thread

Knot positioned
on top of first hole

First pass through
the hole above hole
6, top to bottom.

Then pass
through the
next hole,
bottom to top.

5

Flip the ribbons off the paper. Using a needle
and 1m (40in) thread, go through the first hole
from top to bottom. Loop around and tie a
double knot, positioning it on top of the hole.

6

Pass the needle underneath the loop you have
just made, right to left, and pull the thread
through. Pass under the ribbon, and through
the second hole, going from underneath to top.

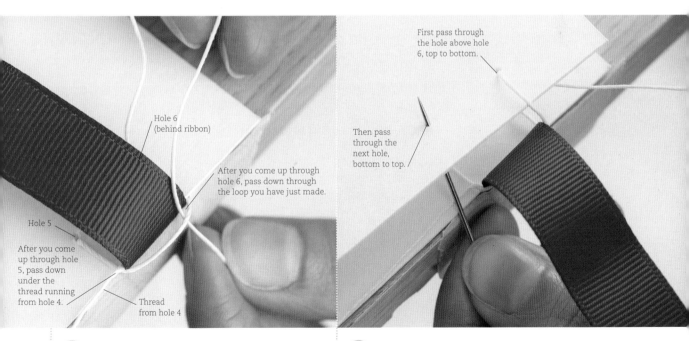

Hole 6
(behind ribbon)

After you come up through
hole 6, pass down through
the loop you have just made.

Hole 5

After you come
up through hole
5, pass down
under the
thread running
from hole 4.

Thread
from hole 4

9

Repeat for holes 5 and 6: pass up through
hole 5, bottom to top, and under the thread
running from hole 4; pass up through hole
6, and down through the loop.

10

Add the second page. Pass through the hole
above hole 6, top to bottom, across the ribbon,
and come up through the next hole. Repeat Steps
7–9 in reverse, but don't go through the last loop.

11

After you come up through the last hole on the second page, pass down through the last loop as well as the loop below it. Add the next page, and pass through the first two holes as in Step 10.

12

Repeat Steps 7–11 for the remaining 13 pages, always passing through both the last loop and the loop below it, securing the loops together in bunches of two. When you run out of thread, attach more with a weaver's knot.

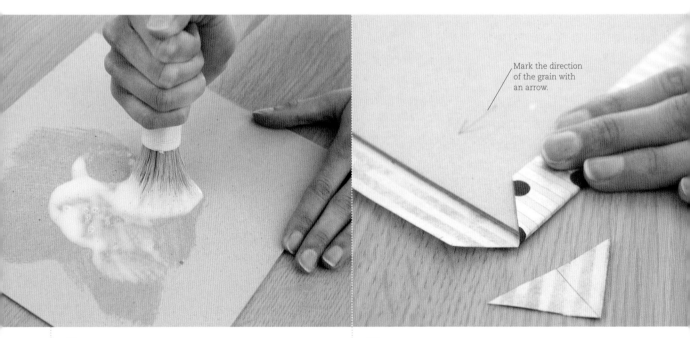

Mark the direction of the grain with an arrow.

14

Cut two cardboard covers, 3mm (⅛in) longer than the pages at the top, bottom, and one side. Cut two sheets of decorative paper, 2cm (¾in) longer on all sides than the boards. Spread glue on each board.

15

With the grain running vertically, place each board, glue side down, in the centre of one sheet of paper. Trim each corner diagonally and glue the edges over the board.

13

With the book closed, push the needle underneath the first page. Open the first page and pull the thread through. Next, push the needle through the first hole on the second page. Turn the page, pull the thread through, and tie a knot on the other side of the second page. Cut the thread.

16

Place one cover on a book the same height as the stack of pages to hold it level and glue down the ribbon ends. Repeat for the other cover, trimming the ribbons if needed.

17

Glue the endpapers to the insides of each board to conceal the ribbons. Place greaseproof paper between both covers and first pages. Weigh down the album and let it dry overnight.

Each of these scented soaps has been made using the method on pp.55–57 and varying the ingredients. See pp.58–59 for variations of the soap recipe.

All natural luxury soap

For the home

Handmade soaps make indulgent gifts, and with the melt-and-pour method require no specialist skill to make. Create naturally scented and coloured soaps using spices, dried fruit or flowers, essential oils, and natural mineral dyes.

To make lemon soap you will need

Tools: gloves • heatproof bowl • pan • spatula • spoon • square mould • knife

Materials: 1kg (2¼lb) white melt-and-pour soap base • ¼–¾ tsp yellow natural mineral colour • dried lemon peel granules • lemon essential oil • surgical spirit in a spray bottle • 9 dried lemon slices • clingfilm

Makes
9 bars

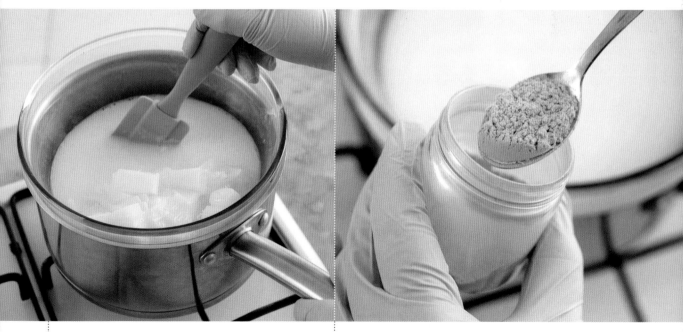

1 Wearing gloves, chop the melt-and-pour soap into pieces and heat in a heatproof bowl over a pan of boiling water, stirring occasionally, until all lumps have melted.

2 Add the desired amount of colouring to the melted soap base and stir until the powder has mixed in and the colour is evenly distributed.

③

Add the lemon peel granules a little at a time, stirring gently. Continue stirring until the granules are spread evenly throughout the soap mixture.

④

Just before you pour the soap mixture into the mould, slowly add the essential oil and stir gently until it is evenly distributed throughout.

⑦

Spray the almost-set layer again with surgical spirit. This will act as a glue and help it to bond to the next layer of soap.

⑧

Slowly pour the remaining mixture into the mould and add the dried lemon slices. You will need to act fast, as the top layer will begin to set as soon as it is poured in.

5

Pour approximately three-quarters of the mixture into the mould. Leave the remainder in the bowl over the hot water to keep it melted and warm.

6

Spray the mixture with surgical spirit to remove any bubbles. Leave this first layer for 20–25 minutes until it is almost set. It should be hard but warm.

9

Create a 3 x 3 pattern so that each slice of soap will contain a lemon slice. Spritz the surface with surgical spirit to remove any bubbles and leave until hard.

10

Remove the soap from the mould and cut it with a knife into nine even squares. Wrap each square in clingfilm to prevent it attracting moisture.

Soap recipe variations

Make a variety of soaps by choosing different scent and colour combinations. All these soaps are made in the same way as the lemon soap (see pp.55–57), using 1kg (2¼lb) of white melt-and-pour soap base and make nine square bars of soap.

A. *Bergamot soap*
¼–¾ tsp orange natural mineral colour
2½ tsp bergamot essential oil
9 whole dried orange slices

B. *Rose soap*
2½ tsp rose absolute diluted in 5% grapeseed oil
100g (3½oz) rose buds

C. *Cinnamon soap*
¼–¾ tsp caramel natural mineral colour
2½ tsp cinnamon leaf essential oil
9 cinnamon sticks

D. *Camomile soap*
¼–¾ tsp dark green natural mineral colour
2½ tsp camomile essential oil
35g (1¼oz) dried camomile flowers

E. *Lavender soap*
¼–¾ tsp purple natural mineral colour
2½ tsp English lavender essential oil
10g (¼oz) dried lavender

F. *Vanilla soap*
¼–¾ tsp cream natural mineral colour
2½ tsp vanilla essential oil
30g (1oz) vanilla pods (use the seeds in the mixture)

G. *Juniper soap*
¼–¾ tsp pink natural mineral colour
2½ tsp juniper essential oil
100g (3½oz) juniper berries

H. *Sandalwood soap*
¼–¾ tsp light brown natural mineral colour
2½ tsp sandalwood fragrance
50g (1¾oz) blue poppy seeds

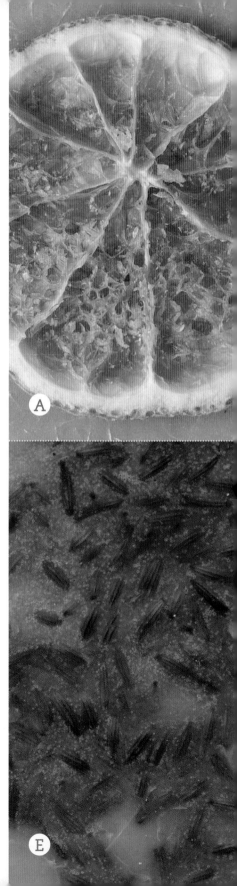

A

E

Manicure
roll

For the home

Use gorgeous Thai silk or pretty cotton for this manicure roll. Fill the pockets with nailcare essentials and add a couple of beautiful polishes to complete the gift. The recipient should feel very pampered!

To make a manicure roll you will need

Tools: dressmaker's scissors • steam iron • sewing machine • sewing pins

Materials: patterned silk-mix fabric • plain silk-mix lining fabric • iron-on interfacing
• ribbon • cotton tape • matching cotton sewing threads

1

Cut one 38 x 43cm (15 x 17in) piece each from the main patterned fabric, the lining fabric, and the iron-on interfacing.

2

Lay the main fabric right-side down and place the interfacing on top. Iron to secure. Machine sew using zigzag or overlock stitch around the edge.

3

Using the zigzag setting, machine sew around the lining fabric to prevent fraying. Place the main and lining fabric together, right sides facing, and sew along the two long edges and one short edge.

4

Turn the fabric right side out. Fold the sides of the open seam inwards. Press and pin. Topstitch along the edge to close.

7

Starting from one of the bottom corners of the pocket, topstitch along the edge, securing the side of the pocket and the ribbon in place. Continue stitching up around the top of the flap, and down the other side, securing the other side of the pocket.

5

Fold the topstitched edge over 11cm (4½in) from the bottom. Cut 41cm (16in) of ribbon and pin it across the pocket, folding and pinning the edges under the pocket.

6

Fold the rest of the ribbon in half and pin the end into the top left corner of the pocket, under the folded edge.

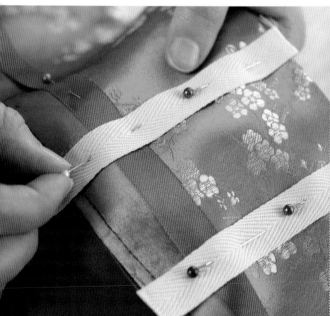

8

Choose how wide you would like the pocket divisions to be and mark them using cotton tape. Pin the tape into position.

9

Machine sew the pockets, using the cotton tape as a guideline. Remove the pins and tape and the manicure roll is ready to fold and tie up with the ribbon tie.

Oilcloth
wash bag

Fill this wash bag with shredded tissue and cosmetics for the perfect pampering gift. The bag is made from oilcloth to make it water resistant, but you could use a sturdy cotton fabric or even quilted cotton for a different look.

To make an oilcloth wash bag you will need

Tools: rotary cutter and mat (or dressmaker's scissors) • sewing pins • sewing machine or needle

Materials: oilcloth • cotton lining fabric • 30cm (12in) zip • cotton sewing thread to match the lining fabric

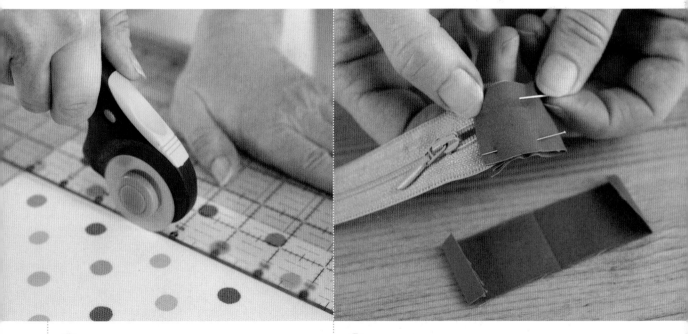

1

Cut two pieces of your chosen outer fabric and two pieces of lining, each 20 x 30cm (8 x 12in). Cut two more pieces of lining fabric, each 9 x 2.5cm (3½ x 1in).

2

Fold over 5mm (¼in) of each end of the small lining strips. Fold one piece over the end of the zip, pin in place, and stitch across all layers. Repeat for the other end.

3

Layer one piece of oilcloth, facing up, with the zip, facing down, and the lining, facing down. Pin. Then pin the other edge of the zip to the other oilcloth and lining pieces in the same way.

4

Stitch through all three layers along each side of the zip, using a long stitch and the correct zip foot for your machine. Make sure that you hold the layers not being stitched out of the way of the needle.

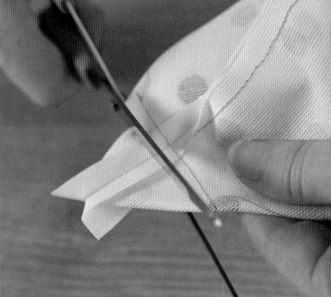

7

Ensure the zip is three-quarters open. Stitch around the edge of the lining and oilcloth, leaving a gap in the lining. When you come to the seams, flatten them to reduce bulk.

8

Shape all four corners by re-folding each corner so that the seam is now in the middle of the new corner. Fold open the seam and stitch across, 3cm (1¼in) up from the corner. Trim off the corner.

5

Use your finger to smooth along the line of the zip, pushing the fabric out. If needed, you can iron the seams on a very low setting, from the lining side protecting it with a tea towel.

6

Next, bring the right sides of the oilcloth and lining pieces together. Pin the two lining pieces together, leaving a 10cm (4in) gap at the bottom edge. You don't need to pin the oilcloth.

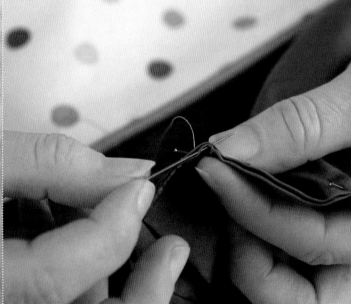

9

Reach through the gap in the lining to turn out the bag, pushing out the corners. If needed, iron on a very low setting from the inside, using a tea towel to protect the bag.

10

Finally, fold under the edges of the gap in the lining, and iron them so that they meet neatly. Then pin and stitch the lining closed either by hand or machine.

Container
candles

A homemade candle can be made into an extra special gift by putting it in a pretty teacup or a handy travel-size tin. Add colour and fragrance to complement the container or the recipient.

To make a teacup candle you will need

Tools: double boiler (or large saucepan and heatproof bowl) • craft thermometer • heat-resistant mat or rack • metal spoon • 2 wooden skewers • 2 elastic bands

Materials: teacup • soy wax flakes (the weight of wax in grams = the volume of water the container holds in ml) • wax dye • wick • wick sustainer

1

Boil water in the lower pan of a double boiler and add wax flakes to the top pan. Alternatively, use a heatproof bowl over a saucepan. Heat the wax, stirring occasionally.

2

When the wax has melted and reached a temperature of 70°C (158°F), take the pan off the heat and add the dye – 1g (¹⁄₁₆oz) for each 100g (3½oz) of wax. Stir until dissolved.

69

3

While the wax is heating, prepare the wick. Attach the wick sustainer (a metal tab) to a length of wick and place in the teacup. Secure the ends of the two skewers with elastic bands and insert the wick between them. Rest the skewers on the rim of the cup and pull the wick gently to ensure it is taut and centred in the cup.

4

Slowly pour the melted wax into the cup and tap it with a spoon to release air bubbles. Allow the candle to cool, add more wax if it has shrunk, then trim the wick when the candle has set.

Scented candles

There are two types of fragrance oil: candle fragrance oil (a synthetic blend) and essential/aromatherapy oil (extracted from plants and flowers, and 100% natural). Both types are stirred into the hot wax just before pouring. Try these different aromatherapy scents to enhance your mood:

A. *Pine or clove*
To increase energy

B. *Lavender or neroli*
To calm, soothe, and relax

C. *Jasmine or bergamot*
To uplift the mood and spirit

D. *Cinnamon or eucalyptus*
To promote concentration

E. *Sandalwood or lemon*
To relieve stress

Travel candles

Handy travel candles can be made in small tins or glass jars with lids.
Create them in the same way as the teacup candle (see pp.69–70).
If you are using different colours or scents, you will need to divide the
hot wax into batches before stirring in the dye or fragrance oil for each
tin. After the candle has set, decorate or label the container as desired.
These candles have each been decorated with beads threaded on a wire
and a label made out of thick foil and embossed from the other side.

Layered candles

To make these layered candles, follow the instructions for making the teacup candle (see pp.69–70). Divide the melted wax into batches – one for each colour you want – and stir in the dyes. With the wick in place, pour the first layer of coloured wax into the glass, tap to release air bubbles, and allow to set. When it is solid to the touch, reheat the next batch of wax and pour in, and repeat for each layer. Leave for 24 hours until fully set.

Tip: Produce darker shades of the same colour by increasing the quantity of dye used in each batch.

Candles in ramekins

Ramekins – small dishes that are usually used for individual pudding portions – are ideal for making a set of candles to give as a gift. The ramekins can be washed and reused as long as the candles have been made with soy wax flakes. (Alternatively, pop them in a freezer for a few hours and the wax should drop out.) Use the method for making the teacup candle on pp.69–70.

Three-wick candle

This impressive three-wick candle can be created in the same way as the teacup candle (see pp.69–70), but you will need another set of skewers to hold the third wick (you should be able to get two wicks into the first set). Multi-wick candles give off more fragrance as well as more light.

Tip: Ceramic bowls or long, narrow plant containers can also be used for multi-wick candles.

For pet lovers

Cat's playmat

For the cat who has everything! This mat will keep your feline friend busy and would also make a luxurious lining for a cat basket, or could be thrown over a favourite chair or sofa. For added appeal, fill the toys with catnip.

To make a cat playmat you will need

Tools: scissors • sewing pins • sewing machine • sewing needle • embroidery hoop

Materials: metallic fabric in orange and silver • thin cord • stuffing • cotton sewing threads • white and black buttons • small bells • feathers • white embroidery thread • wadding • patterned cotton fabric • gingham fabric • orange bias binding • metal rings

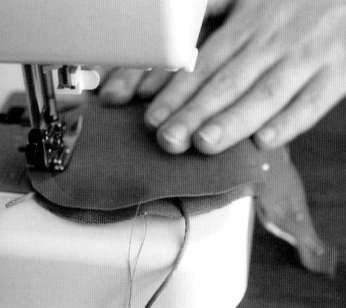

1

Using the template on p.123, cut two sides for each fish from two pieces of orange fabric held right sides together. Pin. Pin the end of 20cm (8in) thin cord to the mouth as shown.

2

Machine sew around the edges, 5mm (¼in) from the edge, securing the cord at the mouth. Leave a 2cm (¾in) gap, allowing the rest of the cord to pass through the gap.

3

Turn the fish right side out. You should have the long length of cord (the "fishing line") hanging from the mouth. Stitch several times through the cord to make it secure.

4

Push stuffing into the fish and sew the opening shut using neat overstitching and matching thread. Repeat to make another fish. Make a fish hook in the same way, using the silver metallic fabric.

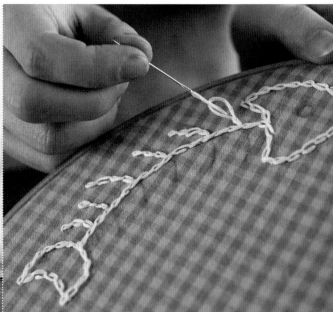

7

Cut a square of gingham fabric and a square of patterned fabric, each 70 x 70cm (27½ x 27½ in). Cut the wadding so it is about 3mm (⅛in) smaller all the way around than the fabric squares.

8

Place the gingham fabric in the embroidery hoop and tighten. Use the template on p.123 to draw a pencil outline of a fish skeleton and use chain stitch and white embroidery thread to go over the design.

 5

Sew a white and black button either side of each fish head. Make sure they are attached securely. Alternatively, embroider eyes using embroidery thread.

 6

Thread and knot a bell to the fishing line about 5cm (2in) from the fish's mouth. Using embroidery thread, tightly bind a feather to the fishing line, just above the bell.

 9

Layer the fabrics – gingham, wadding, then patterned cotton – and pin together. Pin the bias binding around the edge and machine sew through it to sew the layers together.

 10

Attach metal rings to two of the edges and one corner of the mat using cotton thread. Tie the fishes and hook securely to the rings.

Catnip
mice

Filled with catnip, these little mice make a delightful gift that a cat literally cannot resist. This is a great project for using up offcuts and leftover pieces of material. Cotton fabrics work well, but why not also try tweed or leather?

To make a catnip mouse you will need

Tools: dressmaker's scissors • pencil • sewing pins • sewing machine • sewing needle
Materials: cotton fabric • felt fabric in two different colours • white wool yarn • wadding • cotton sewing thread • dried catnip (optional) • black embroidery thread

1

Using the template on p.125, cut out two main body pieces from two pieces of fabric held right sides together. Cut out the base and ears from coloured felt.

2

Cut three lengths of wool to twice as long as you would like the tail to be and knot them together. Knot the short ends around a pencil and make a plait to use for the tail.

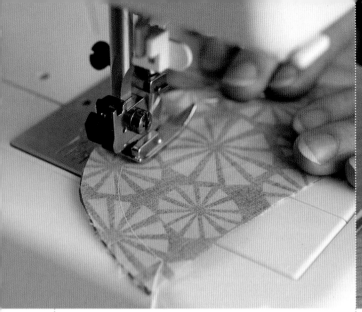

3

Pin the body pieces together, right side to right side. Start sewing 8mm (⅜in) in from the bottom edge. Sew around the curve, stopping 8mm (⅜in) from the end.

4

Tie off the ends and trim the excess fabric to make the seam less bulky once the mouse is turned right side out.

7

Trim off the excess fabric in the seams and turn the mouse right side out, pushing the nose out with your finger. If necessary, use a needle to pull out the tip from the outside.

8

Push small amounts of wadding into the mouse, ensuring that you fill the nose. When it is half stuffed, add dried catnip. Finish stuffing the mouse.

5

Pin the felt base to the long sides of the body pieces, so that the right side of each of the pieces is facing the felt base.

6

Starting from the back end (the slightly raised end) of the mouse, stitch all the way around the sides, attaching the top layer to the base, and stopping 2.5cm (1in) before the end.

9

Insert the tail underneath the back seam, pinning the seam closed. Using small stitches, carefully sew up the opening, securing the tail into position.

10

Bring one cut edge of the ear over the other so that the ear curves inward. Pin in place and stitch down, repeating for the other side. Embroider two black eyes onto the mouse.

Simple silhouette

An even easier way to create an appliqué keepsake of your pet is to cut out a side-on silhouette from one fabric. Do this by enlarging a profile photograph on a photocopier to use as a template. You can make this floral pup using the template on p.125.

Appliqué
pet portrait

Use the appliqué technique to create a stunning portrait of a beloved pet, perfect for decorating a cushion or displaying in a frame. Use the cat template provided, or make your own from a favourite photograph.

To make an appliqué pet portrait cushion cover you will need

Tools: iron • dressmaker's scissors • sewing needle • sewing pins • sewing machine
Materials: bonding web • black, grey, and white fabric • cushion cover
• contrast cotton sewing thread for tacking • blue, pink, and black felt • black and white cotton sewing thread

1
Re-size the template (see p.124) to fit your cushion cover. Transfer the head piece on to bonding web, and iron it on to the reverse of your selected fabric.

2
Repeat the process for the back, chest, ear, and muzzle pieces. Then cut out each element. Note that the eyes and nose don't need to be faced.

3

Carefully peel off the backing paper from all the faced pieces.

4

Assemble the pieces on the cushion cover. Make sure the head piece overlaps the chest piece and the back piece. Iron in place.

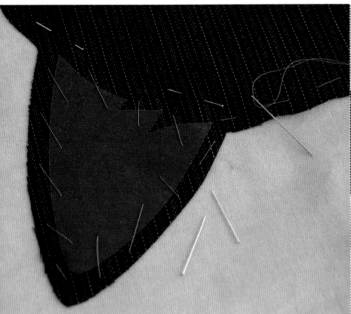
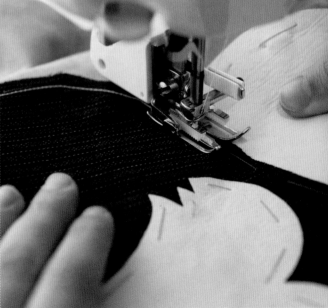

7

Pin, then tack the pieces, except the eyes and nose, in place on the cushion cover. Remove the pins.

8

Sew around the outside of each of the tacked pieces about 5mm (¼in) from the edge, either by hand or with a sewing machine. Remove the tacking thread.

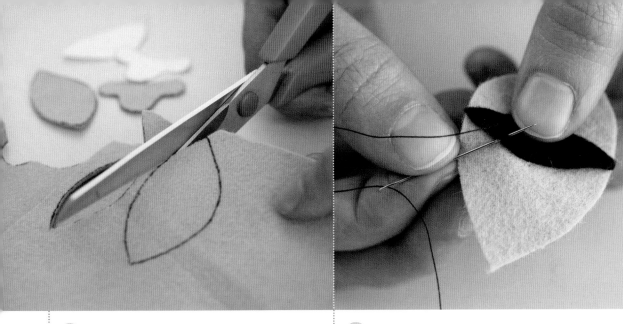

 5

Trace the eyes, nose, and pupils on to coloured felt and cut them out.

 6

Stitch pupils on to the eye pieces using tiny backstitches and black thread.

 9

Tack the eyes and nose on to the cat's face and stitch around the edges of each piece. Remove the tacking thread.

10

Using the image on p.84 as a guide, sew guidelines for the whiskers and eyelashes using tacking thread. Stitch over them using topstitch. Remove the tacking threads.

Tartan
dog jacket

For pet lovers

Keep a favourite dog warm and cosy all winter long with this easy-to-make, fleece-lined jacket. You can adjust the pattern to make it in any size. It fastens with Velcro, making it easy to put on and take off.

To make a tartan dog jacket you will need

Tools: tracing paper • dressmaker's scissors • sewing pins • sewing machine
Materials: tartan check fabric • wadding • interfacing • fleece fabric • cotton sewing threads
• Velcro • red grosgrain ribbon

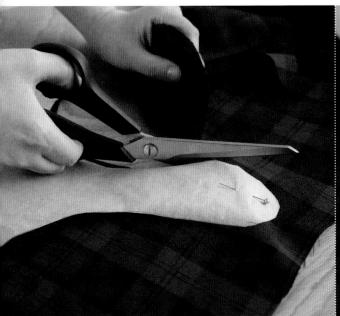

1
Using the template on pp.126-27, use tracing paper to make a pattern and adjust it to fit your dog. Cut out one jacket piece and one belly strap from each fabric.

2
Place the check fabric, right side out, on top of the wadding and interfacing. Pin all three layers together.

89

3

Machine sew along the lines of the
check fabric using a long stitch, first
in one direction and then the other.
This quilts the jacket.

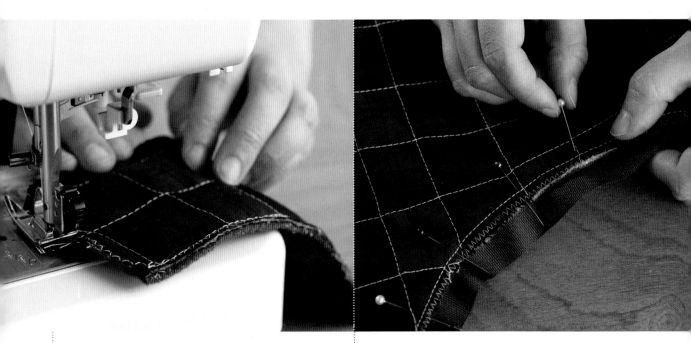

6

Machine sew around the edges of
the jacket, joining the upper and
lining pieces. Neaten the edges
with a zigzag or overlock stitch.

7

Pin the grosgrain ribbon around the jacket
as shown. Machine sew around the ribbon to
attach. Fold the other half of the ribbon over
the edge, and topstitch or hand stitch to attach.

4

Pin Velcro onto the lining and the quilted upper at the points marked on the template. Stitch the Velcro into place.

5

Pin the quilted upper and the fleece lining together, right sides out.

8

Make the belly strap in the same way as the jacket, attaching Velcro to the belly strap as indicated on the template. Pin the two sections as shown and stitch together.

Gift wrap

Square
gift box

A gift box is the ideal way to present awkwardly shaped gifts. You can make this gift box exactly the required size by re-sizing the template. Use patterned card, or glue decorative paper to card before you start to create different looks.

To make a square gift box you will need

Tools: pencil • scalpel • cutting mat • ruler • blunt knife (or pair of scissors) • rubber
Materials: patterned card (or patterned paper glued onto card) • tracing paper • glue stick

1
Use a photocopier to re-size the box stencil on p.97. Using tracing paper and a pencil, transfer the template onto patterned card (or glue patterned paper to the back of the card).

2
Using a scalpel and a cutting mat, carefully cut out the shape you have drawn. Take care not to cut into the internal folding lines.

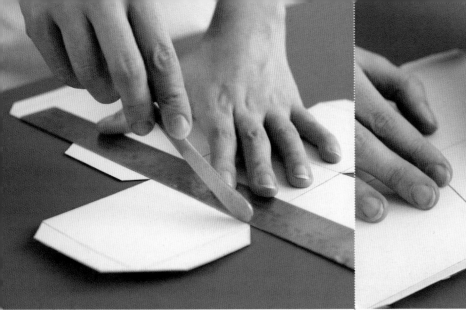

3

Once you have cut out the entire shape, score all the folding lines using a ruler and blunt knife, or one side of a pair of scissors. This will make the box easier to assemble.

4

Fold the sides inwards along the scored lines, making sure that each crease is sharp. For a neat finish, rub out the pencil lines along the creases inside the box.

5

Attach the three sides not adjacent to the lid to each other using the glue stick or double-sided sticky tape on the outside of the flaps. Hold in place until set.

6

Fold in the flaps of the last remaining side, spread glue or attach tape to the patterned side of the flaps, and slot the side into place. Press the flaps down, and hold in place until set.

Square gift box template

Please enlarge to the required
size on a photocopier

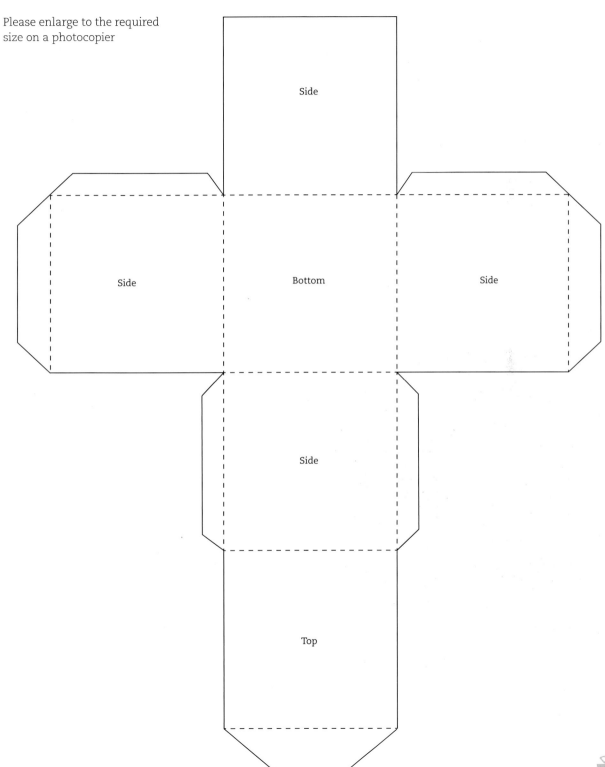

Side

Side

Bottom

Side

Side

Top

Homemade
gift bags

Follow this simple tutorial to turn any sheet of wrapping paper or gift wrap into a bespoke gift bag. For an even more personalized bag, use a sheet of paper printed with a message, or even a printout of a photograph.

To make a gift bag you will need

Tools: pencil • scissors • blunt knife (or pair of scissors) • glue stick • hole punch

Materials: tracing paper • wrapping paper or other printed or plain paper • card • ribbon

1

Re-size the template from pp.102-103 to the required size on a photocopier. Using tracing paper and a pencil, transfer the template onto the wrong side of your chosen paper.

2

Cut out the bag shape along the outer lines. Take care to not cut along any of the internal folding lines.

3

Score along the horizontal top and bottom folding lines, using a ruler and a blunt knife (or one side of a pair of scissors). Fold down the bottom and top flaps, making sure the creases are sharp.

4

Score along each of the vertical folding lines, going across the top and bottom flaps. Then fold the bag in along each of these lines in turn, again making sharp creases.

7

Fold the bottom of the bag as if you were wrapping a present. Fold one long side of the bottom tab in across the opening, creasing the sides sharply. Fold the sides in over the opening, again creasing sharply. Finally, fold in the remaining side to cover the opening, and glue or tape the base down.

5

Using a glue stick, spread glue evenly along the top flap. Smooth it down, holding it in place until it sticks. This will help the bag hold its shape.

6

Fold out the bottom flap. Spread glue along the outside of the side tab, and attach it to the inside of the opposite end, all the way along its length. Glue the other side tab over the seam.

8

Cut out a piece of card the size of the base of the bag, and place it in the bottom of the bag. This will strengthen the base.

9

Using a two-hole punch (or a single-hole punch), punch two holes on each long side of the bag, through the centre of the reinforced top fold. Add ribbon for handles.

Gift bag template

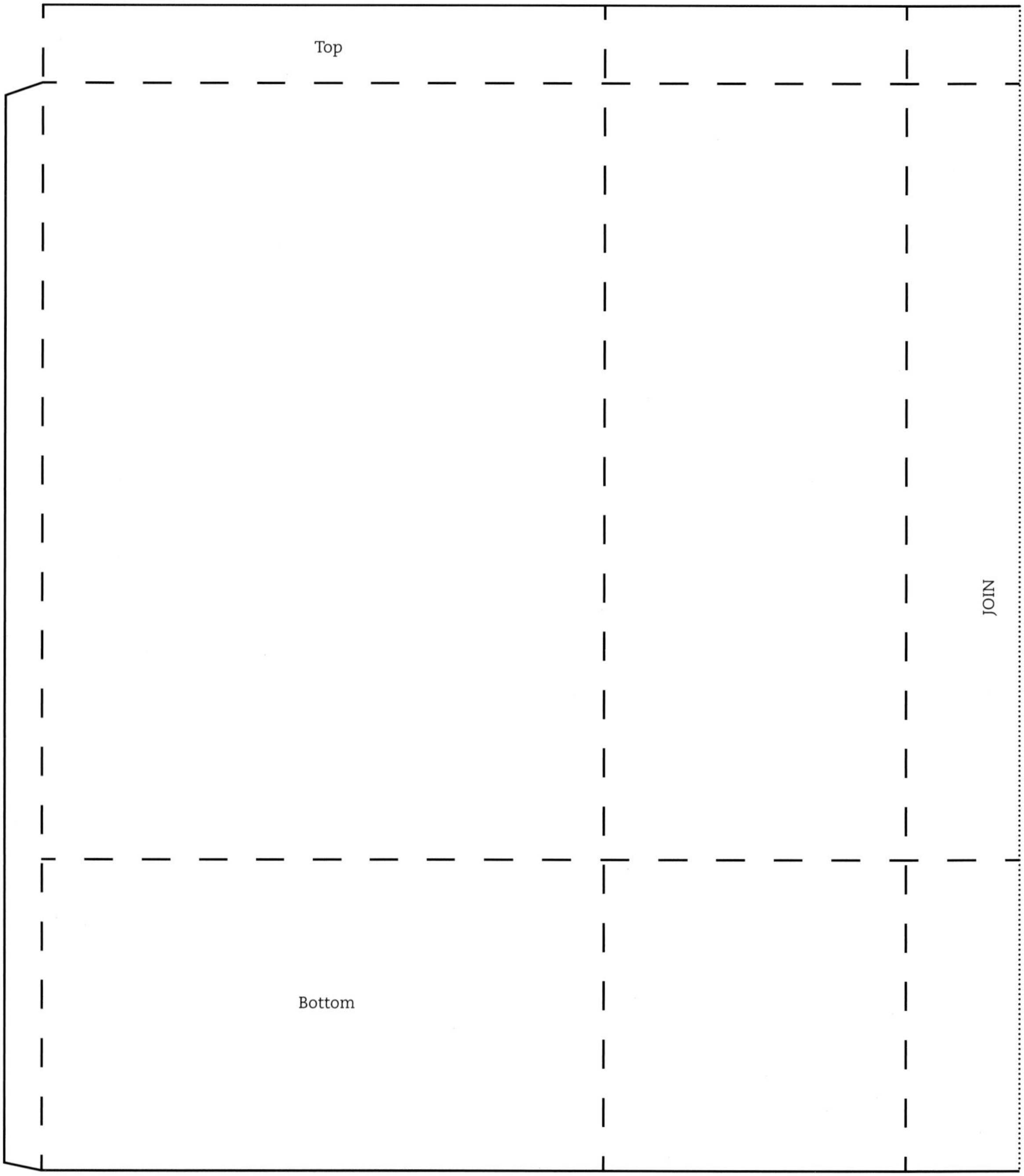

Top

JOIN

Bottom

JOIN

Side
tab

Twist-top gift box

This ingenious gift box comes complete with its own closing mechanism – specially shaped flaps twist and lock together to hide your surprise inside. Perfect for wrapping up homemade sweets or jewellery in style.

To make a twist-top gift box you will need

Tools: pencil • scalpel • cutting mat • ruler • blunt knife (or pair of scissors)
Materials: card • tracing paper • decorative paper or wrapping paper • glue stick

1
Use a photocopier to re-size the twist-top box template on pp.108-09, if required. Use tracing paper and a pencil to transfer the pattern onto a sheet of card.

2
Glue a sheet of wrapping paper or decorative paper to the reverse of the card. Alternatively, you could use patterned card to make the box.

3

Using a scalpel and cutting mat, carefully cut around the pattern. First cut along the outermost lines of the template.

4

Next, using the template on pp.108-09 as a guide, cut into the shape along the lines marked as cutting lines. Finally, remove the small shapes in the top as marked.

6

Fold all the scored lines as marked, ensuring that all the creases are sharp. Assemble the body of the box by gluing both side flaps to the opposite side of the box.

5

Using a ruler and a blunt knife (or one side of a pair of scissors) score all the dashed lines from the wrong side of the card. Score the lines marked with dashes and dots from the right side of the card.

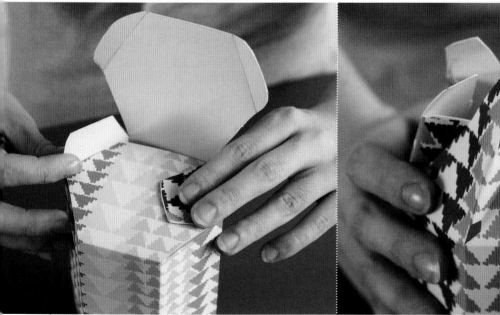

7

Assemble the base of the box by first folding in the piece marked Base 1. Next fold down the two base flaps, and finally Base 2, tucking the attached flaps into the box.

8

Ensure that each of the creases made to the top part of the box is creased in the correct direction. Fill the box and push the flaps down and towards the centre to seal it.

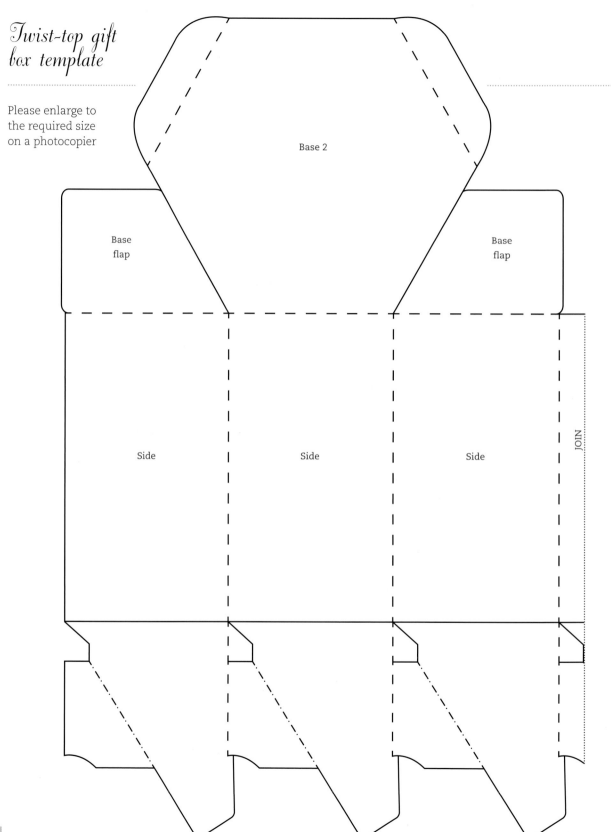

Twist-top gift box template

Please enlarge to the required size on a photocopier

Base 2

Base flap

Base flap

Side

Side

Side

JOIN

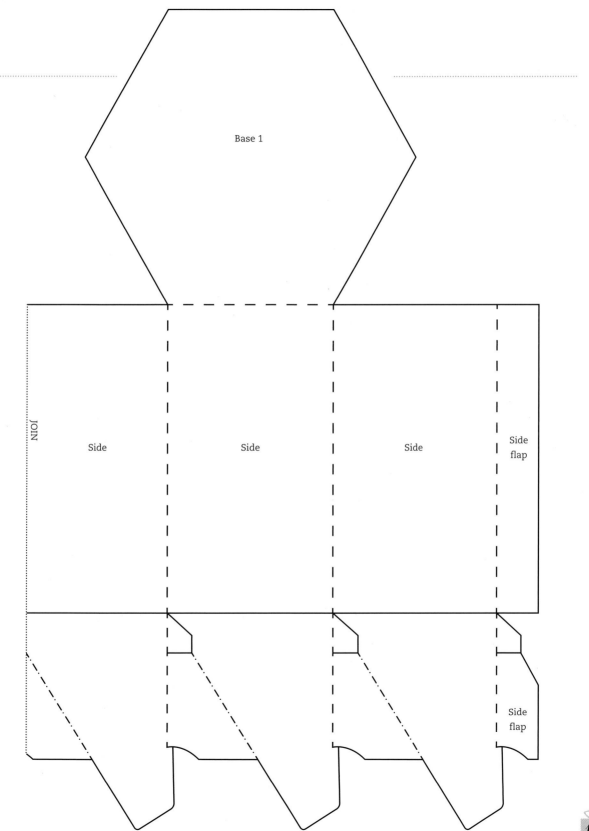

Base 1

JOIN

Side

Side

Side

Side flap

Side flap

Printed
gift wrap

Gift wrap

Making your own gift wrap finishes off any gift with a personal touch. This stamped pattern of blocks of stripes is easy to create. Once you have mastered this technique, why not try creating your own shapes and patterns?

To make printed gift wrap you will need

Tools: scissors • glue

Materials: wood or balsa wood block • foam board • inkpad • sheets of white paper

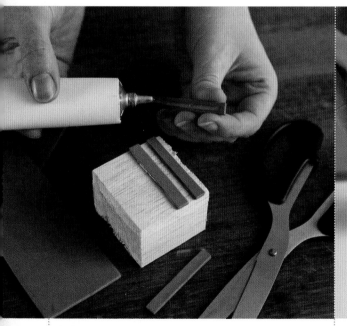

1

To make a line stamp, start with a wooden block. Cut out strips of the desired width from foam board. Glue the strips to one side of a block and allow the glue to dry.

2

To make line-printed gift wrap, press the stamp on an inkpad and stamp in one corner of a sheet of paper. Continue stamping the paper, alternating the orientation of the stamp, until the paper is filled.

Templates

Blossom cushion (pp.8–11)

Please enlarge to the required
size on a photocopier

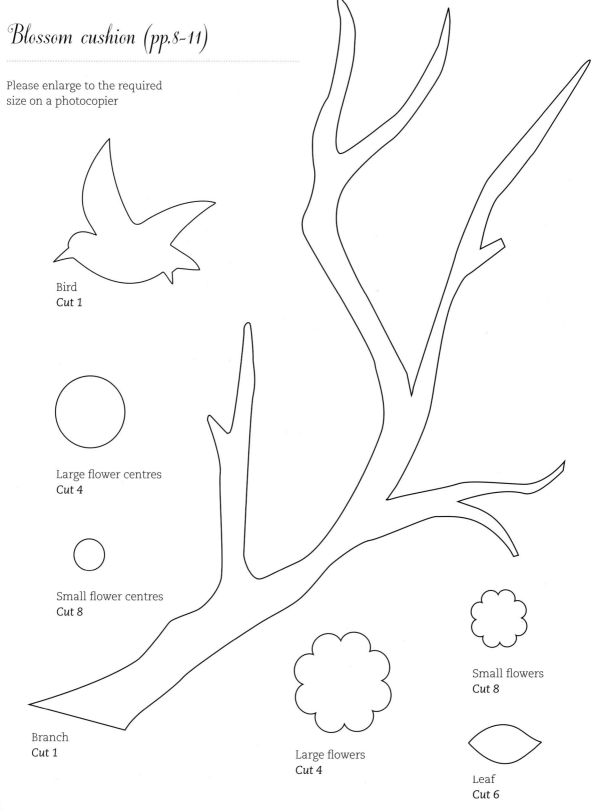

Bird
Cut 1

Large flower centres
Cut 4

Small flower centres
Cut 8

Branch
Cut 1

Large flowers
Cut 4

Small flowers
Cut 8

Leaf
Cut 6

Skull and crossbones cushion (p. 13)

Please enlarge to the required size on a photocopier

Eyes
Cut 1 of each

Teeth
Cut 1

Skull
Cut 1

Crossbones
Cut 1

Guitar cushion (p. 13)

Please enlarge to the required size on a photocopier

Guitar inset
Cut 1

Dial
Cut 3

Pickup
Cut 3

Neck
Cut 1

Guitar
Cut 1

Bridge
Cut 1

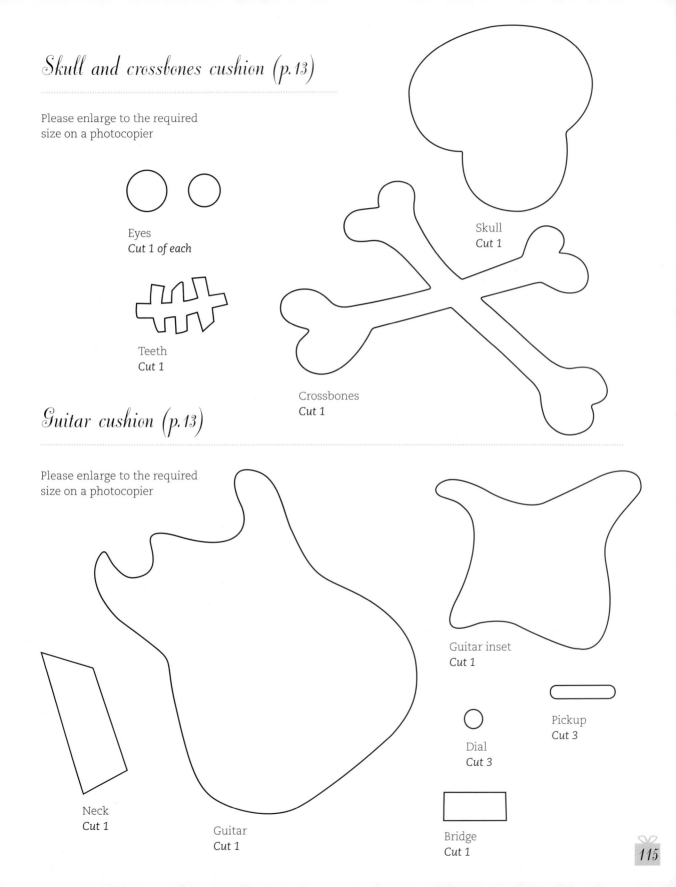

115

Castle cushion (p.12)

Please enlarge to the required size on a photocopier

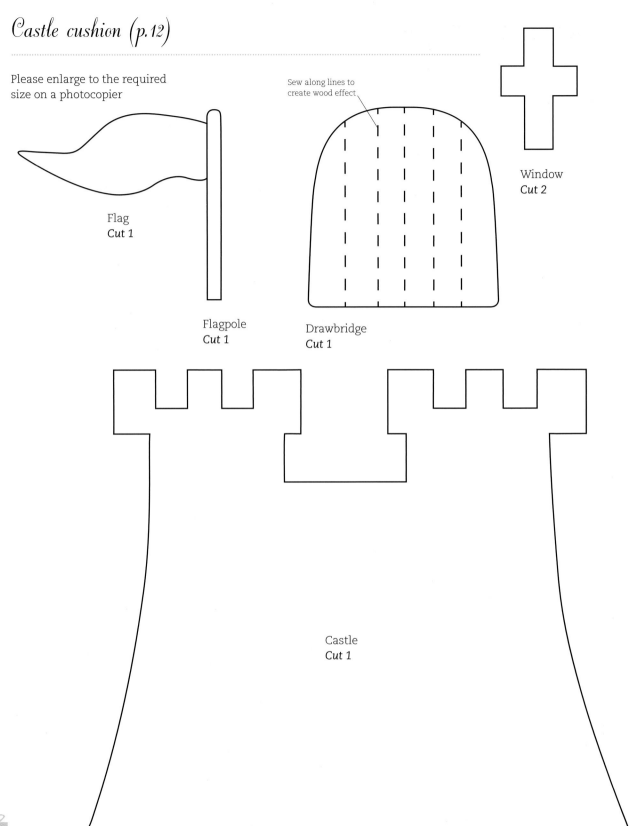

Flag
Cut 1

Flagpole
Cut 1

Sew along lines to create wood effect

Drawbridge
Cut 1

Window
Cut 2

Castle
Cut 1

Castle cushion dolls (p.12)

Please enlarge to the required
size on a photocopier

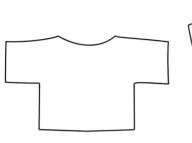

Prince's top
Cut 2
*If making the clothes out of felt, place pieces around doll and
sew together from the outside. If using other fabric, add a seam
allowance, sew together with right sides facing, and turn.*

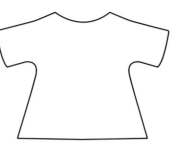

Princess's dress
Cut 2

Body
*Cut 2 for each doll.
Sew together along
the edges, leaving a
gap. Turn, stuff, and
sew the gap closed.*

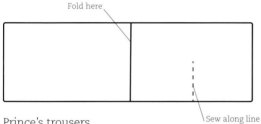

Fold here

Sew along line
through all layers
to make legs

Prince's trousers
Cut 1
Wrap around doll and sew in place.

Crown
*Wrap around head
and sew in place.*

Rollaway gameboard (pp.26–31)

Type of fabric	Cut	Measurements in cm and in
Board: dark fabric	x 5	5 x 40cm (2 x 16in)
Board: light fabric	x 5	5 x 40cm (2 x 16in)
Outer fabric	x 1	30 x 50cm (12 x 20in)
Inner fabric	x 2	30 x 14cm (12 x 5¾in)
Inner fabric	x 2	5 x 27cm (2 x 10¾in)
Interfacing	x 1	30 x 50cm (12 x 20in)
Interfacing	x 1	30 x 14cm (12 x 5¾in)

Please enlarge to the required
size on a photocopier

Dot-decorated mug and coaster set (p. 18)

Dot-decorated bunting plate (p. 19)

Please enlarge to the required size on a photocopier

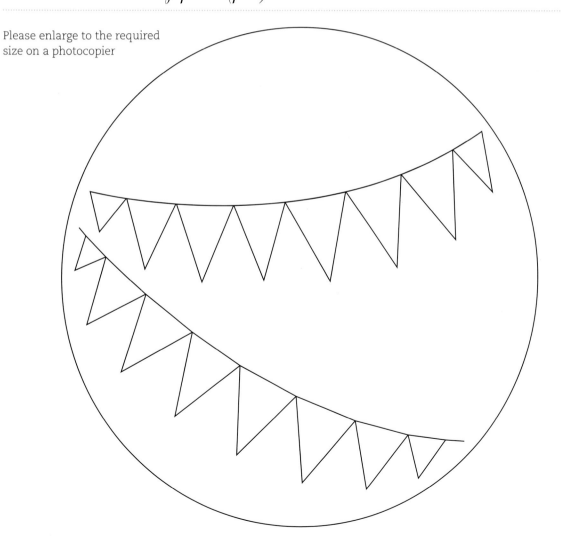

Stencilled bags (pp.32-37)

Please enlarge to the required
size on a photocopier

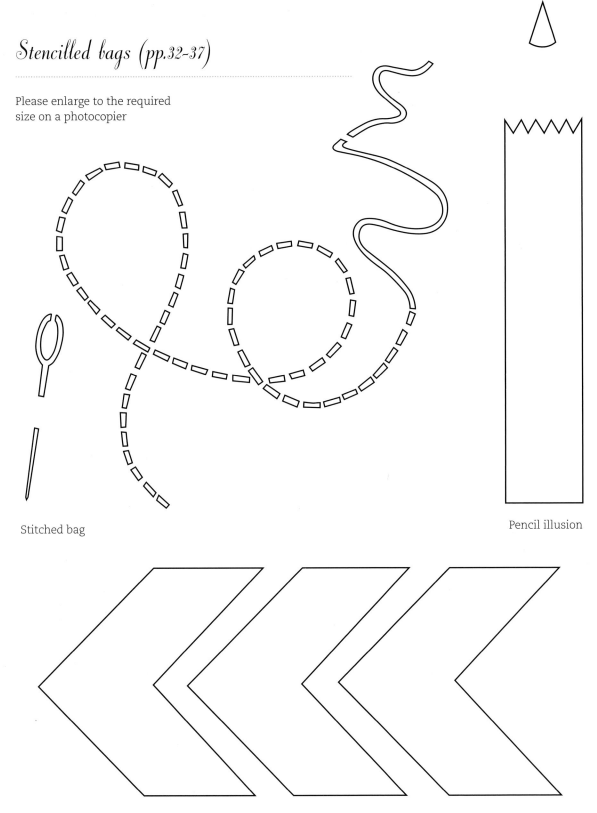

Stitched bag

Pencil illusion

Repeated chevrons

Fluttering butterflies

Wave

Ribbon-bound photo album (pp.48-53)

Please enlarge to the required
size on a photocopier

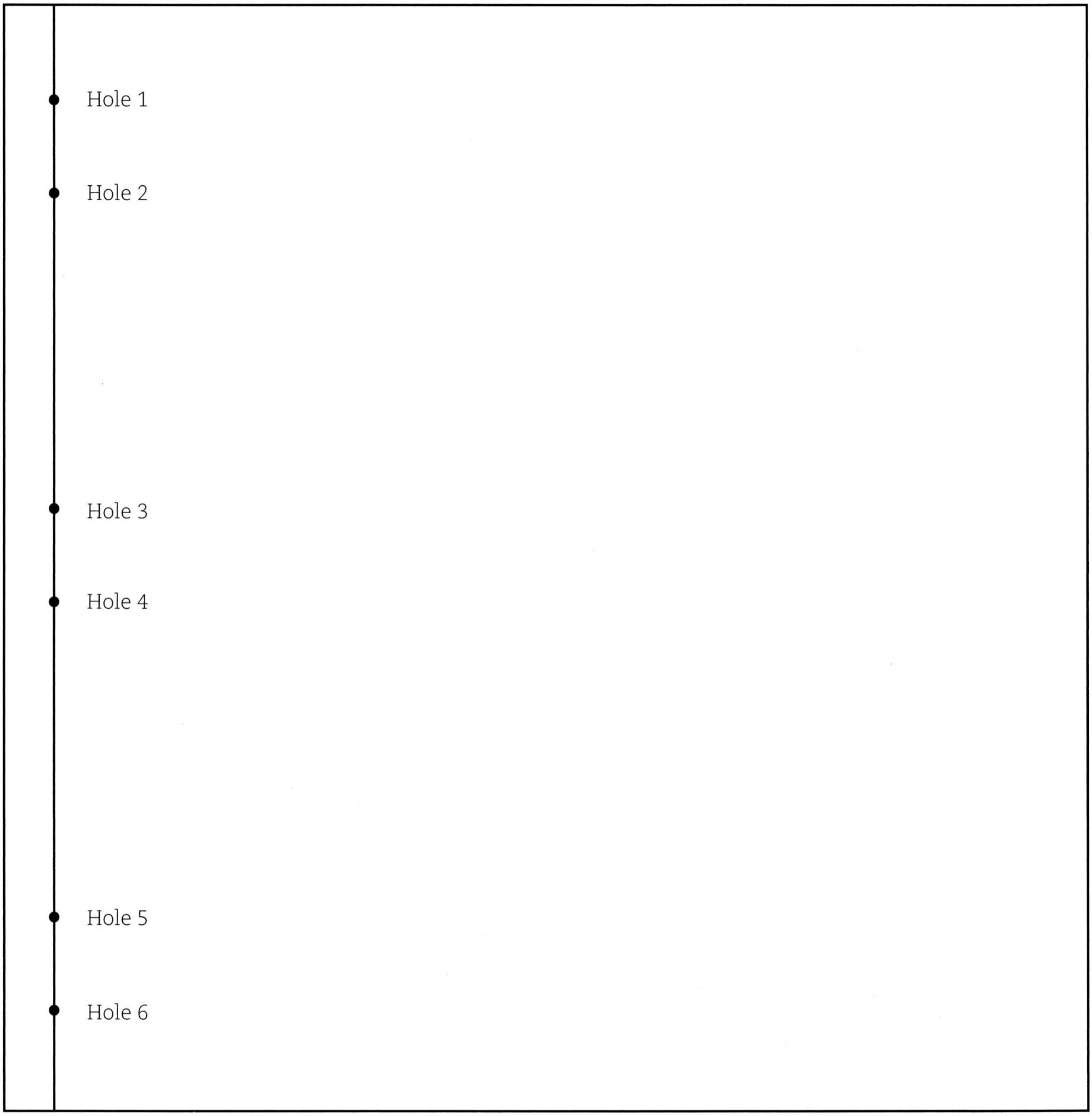

Hole 1

Hole 2

Hole 3

Hole 4

Hole 5

Hole 6

Cat's playmat (pp.76–79)

Please enlarge to the required
size on a photocopier

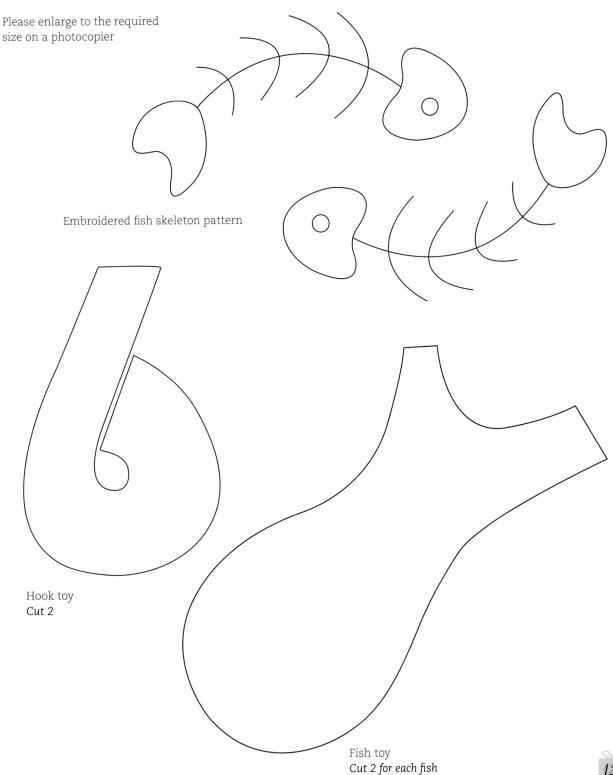

Embroidered fish skeleton pattern

Hook toy
Cut 2

Fish toy
Cut 2 for each fish

Appliqué pet portrait (pp.84–87)

Please enlarge to the required
size on a photocopier

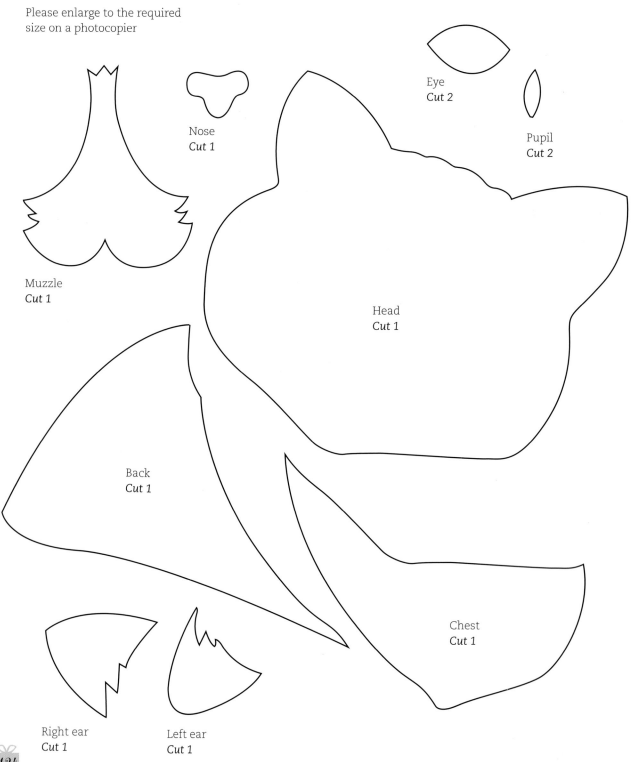

Nose
Cut 1

Eye
Cut 2

Pupil
Cut 2

Muzzle
Cut 1

Head
Cut 1

Back
Cut 1

Chest
Cut 1

Right ear
Cut 1

Left ear
Cut 1

Simple silhouette pet portrait (p.84)

Please enlarge to the required
size on a photocopier

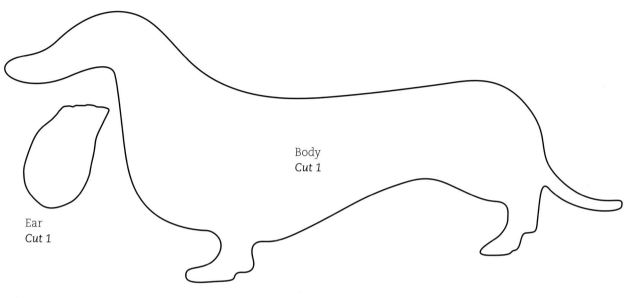

Body
Cut 1

Ear
Cut 1

Catnip mice (pp.80–83)

Please enlarge to the required
size on a photocopier

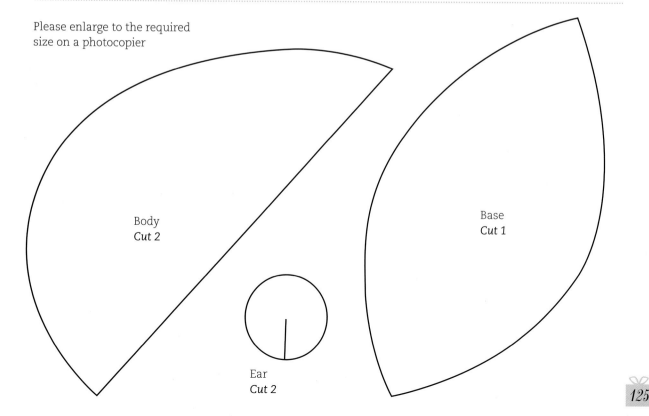

Body
Cut 2

Ear
Cut 2

Base
Cut 1

Tartan dog jacket (pp.88–91)

Please enlarge to the required
size on a photocopier

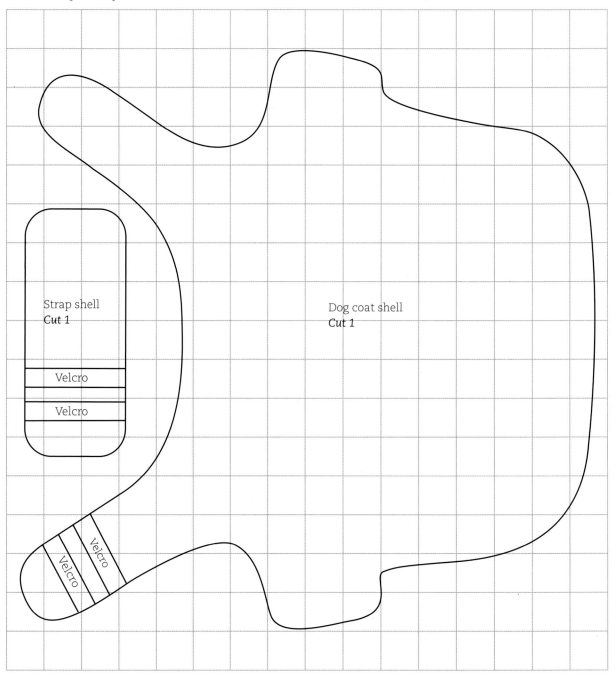

Strap shell
Cut 1

Velcro

Velcro

Dog coat shell
Cut 1

Velcro

Velcro

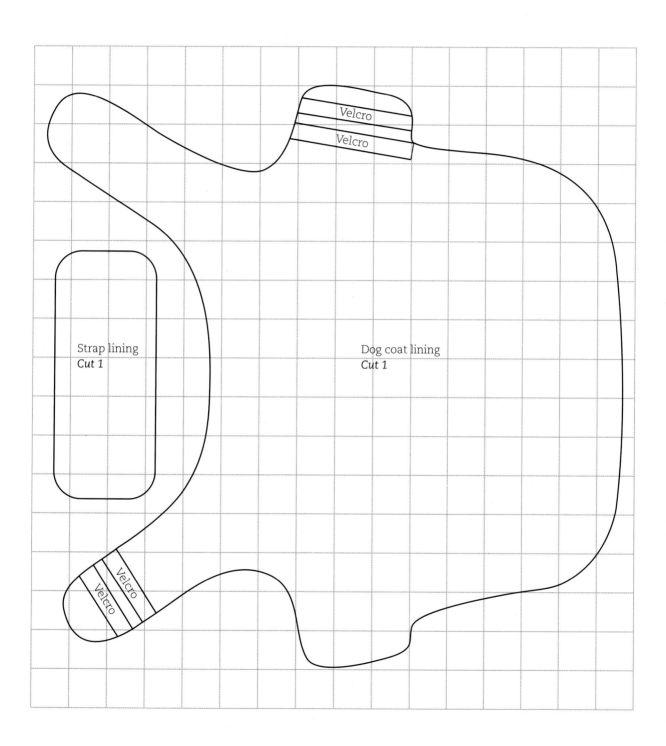

Velcro

Velcro

Strap lining
Cut 1

Dog coat lining
Cut 1

Velcro

Velcro

Dorling Kindersley would like to thank the following people for their hard work and contributions towards *Handmade Home*:

Project makers

Hannah Moore: Customized cushion p.8, Guitar cushion p.13, Skull and Crossbones cushion p.13, Rollaway gameboard p.26, Cat's playmat p.76, Catnip mice p.80, Appliqué pet portrait p.84, **Caroline Stamps:** Oilcloth wash bag p.64; **Isobel Cordova:** Travel candle p.71; Layered candle p.72, Candles in ramekins p.72, Three-wick candle p.73; **The Oxford Soap Company:** All-natural luxury soaps p.54; **Ria Holland:** Dot-decorated ceramics p.14, Mug and coaster set p.18, Celebration bunting plate p.19; **Paula Keogh:** Manicure roll p.60, Tartan dog jacket p.88; **Nicola Barter:** Stencilled bags pp.32-37; **Victoria Read:** Personalized journal p.42, Ribbon-bound photo album p.48; **Lova Rajaonarimanana:** Phone and tablet protectors p.38; **Karen Mitchell:** Mosaic bowl p.20, Flower garldand mirror p.24, Owl jewellery box p.24, Round tealight holder p.25, Seaside coasters p.25; **Charlotte Johnson:** Square gift box p.94, Homemade gift bags p.98, Twist-top gift box p104; **Helen Fickling:** Teacup candle p.68.

2013 Handmade Gifts

DK UK Project Art Editor Gemma Fletcher; **Project Editor** Laura Palosuo; **Designer** Charlotte Johnson; **Photographer** Dave King; Managing Editor Penny Smith; Managing Art Editor Marianne Markham **DK INDIA Senior Art Editor** Ivy Roy; **Art Editor** Vikas Sachdeva; **Assistant Art Editor** Pallavi Kapur; **Managing Art Editor** Navidita Thapa.